ANIMALS THAT LIVE ON THE FARM
ANIMALES QUE VIVEN EN LA GRANJA

Horses/ Los caballos

JoAnn Early Macken

Reading consultant/Consultora de lectura:
Susan Nations, M.Ed.,
author/literacy coach/consultant

WEEKLY WR READER®
EARLY LEARNING LIBRARY

O4O5J123

Please visit our web site at: www.earlyliteracy.cc
For a free color catalog describing Weekly Reader® Early Learning Library's list
of high-quality books, call 1-877-445-5824 (USA) or 1-800-387-3178 (Canada).
Weekly Reader® Early Learning Library's fax: (414) 336-0164.

Library of Congress Cataloging-in-Publication Data available upon request from publisher.
Fax (414) 336-0157 for the attention of the Publishing Records Department.

ISBN 0-8368-4288-X (lib. bdg.)
ISBN 0-8368-4295-2 (softcover)

This edition first published in 2005 by
Weekly Reader® Early Learning Library
330 West Olive Street, Suite 100
Milwaukee, WI 53212 USA

Copyright © 2005 by Weekly Reader® Early Learning Library

Picture research: Diane Laska-Swanke
Art direction: Tammy West
Cover design and page layout: Kami Koenig
Translators: Colleen Coffey and Consuelo Carrillo

Photo credits: Cover, pp. 9, 19 Gregg Andersen; pp. 5, 7 © Daniel Johnson;
p. 11 © Alan & Sandy Carey; pp. 13, 15, 17 © Sharon Eide and Elizabeth
Flynn/SandEphoto.com; p. 21 © James P. Rowan

Printed in the United States of America

1 2 3 4 5 6 7 8 9 08 07 06 05 04

Note to Educators and Parents

Reading is such an exciting adventure for young children! They are beginning to integrate their oral language skills with written language. To encourage children along the path to early literacy, books must be colorful, engaging, and interesting; they should invite the young reader to explore both the print and the pictures.

Animals That Live on the Farm is a new series designed to help children read about the behavior and life cycles of farm animals. Each book describes a different type of animal and explains why and how it is raised.

Each book is specially designed to support the young reader in the reading process. The familiar topics are appealing to young children and invite them to read — and re-read — again and again. The full-color photographs and enhanced text further support the student during the reading process.

In addition to serving as wonderful picture books in schools, libraries, homes, and other places where children learn to love reading, these books are specifically intended to be read within an instructional guided reading group. This small group setting allows beginning readers to work with a fluent adult model as they make meaning from the text. After children develop fluency with the text and content, the book can be read independently. Children and adults alike will find these books supportive, engaging, and fun!

Una nota a los educadores y a los padres

¡La lectura es una emocionante aventura para los niños! En esta etapa están comenzando a integrar su manejo del lenguaje oral con el lenguaje escrito. Para fomentar la lectura desde una temprana edad, los libros deben ser vistosos, atractivos e interesantes; deben invitar al joven lector a explorar tanto el texto como las ilustraciones.

Animales que viven en la granja es una nueva serie pensada para ayudar a los niños a conocer la conducta y los ciclos de vida de los animales de la granja. Cada libro describe un tipo diferente de animal y explica por qué y cómo se cria.

Cada libro ha sido especialmente diseñado para facilitar el proceso de lectura. La familiaridad con los temas tratados atrae la atención de los niños y los invita a leer — y releer — una y otra vez. Las fotografías a todo color y el tipo de letra facilitan aún más al estudiante el proceso de lectura.

Además de servir como fantásticos libros ilustrados en la escuela, la biblioteca, el hogar y otros lugares donde los niños aprenden a amar la lectura, estos libros han sido concebidos específicamente para ser leídos en grupos de instrucción guiada. Este contexto de grupos pequeños permite que los niños que se inician en la lectura trabajen con un adulto cuya fluidez les sirve de modelo para comprender el texto. Una vez que se han familiarizado con el texto y el contenido, los niños pueden leer los libros por su cuenta. ¡Tanto niños como adultos encontrarán que estos libros son útiles, entretenidos y divertidos!

— Susan Nations, M.Ed., author, literacy coach,
and consultant in literacy development

A baby horse is called a **foal**. A foal can stand soon after it is born.

Un caballo recién nacido se llama **potro**. Un potro puede sostenerse en pie al poco tiempo de nacido.

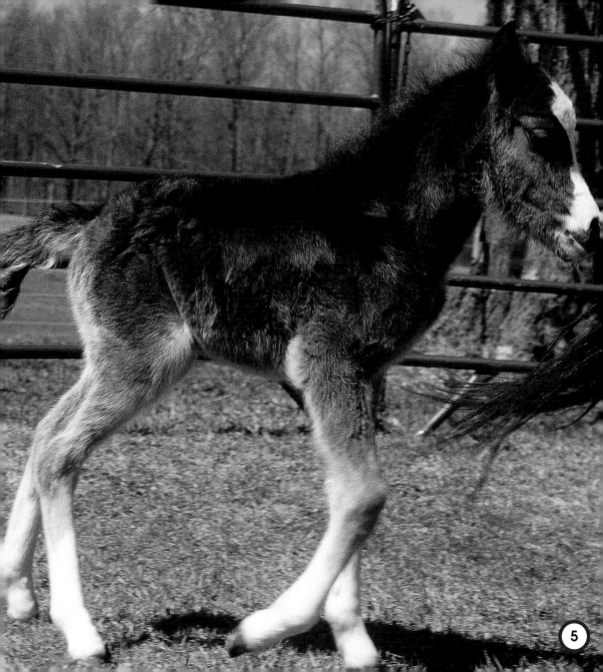

A foal drinks its mother's milk. In a few weeks, it grazes on grass.

- - - - - - - -

El potro se alimenta con la leche de la madre. Después de algunas semanas, pasta la hierba.

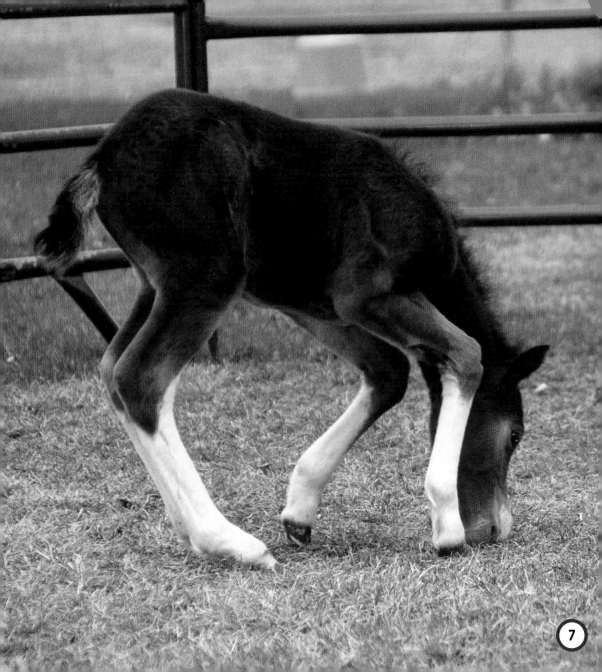

Horses also eat hay and grain. They need fresh water and shelter.

– – – – – – – –

Los caballos comen heno y grano también. Necesitan agua fresca y refugio.

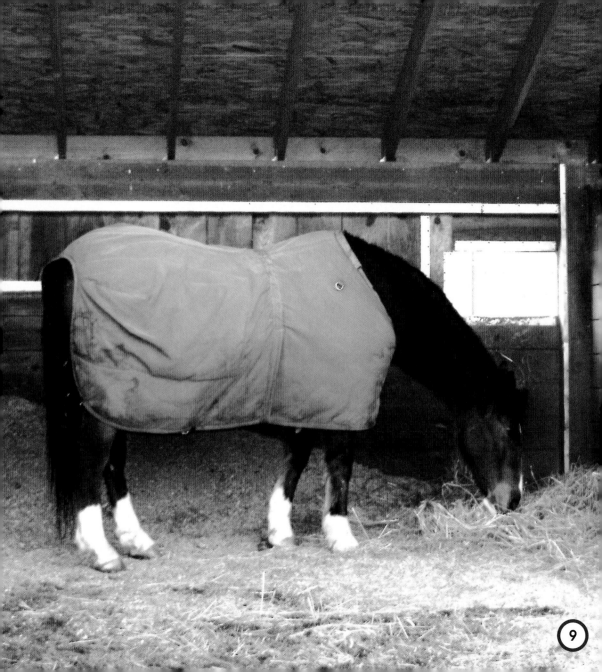

When a horse is one year old, it is a **yearling**. It can learn to carry a rider.

- - - - - - - -

Cuando el caballo tiene un año, se llama **potranco**. Puede aprender a llevar un jinete.

Horses walk, trot, and **gallop**, or run. Horses can sleep standing up.

– – – – – – – –

Los caballos caminan, trotan y **galopan** o corren. Los caballos pueden dormir parados.

A horse's eyes are on the sides of its head. Horses can see ahead and to the sides. They can even see behind them!

— — — — — — — —

Los ojos del caballo están a los lados de la cabeza. Los caballos pueden ver hacia adelante y hacia los lados. ¡Incluso pueden ver detrás de ellos!

Horses hear very well, too.
Their ears can turn toward
sounds.

- - - - - - - -

También los caballos oyen
muy bien. Las orejas se
orientan en dirección a los
sonidos.

Some horses are only as tall as a desk. Some are as tall as a door. A large horse can weigh a ton.

- - - - - - - -

Algunos caballos son tan pequeños como un escritorio. Otros son tan altos como una puerta. Un caballo grande puede pesar una tonelada.

Some farmers use horses for work. Have you ever seen horses on a farm?

— — — — — — —

Algunos granjeros usan los caballos para trabajar. ¿Alguna vez has visto caballos en una granja?

Glossary/Glosario

grain — seeds or fruit from grass plants
grano — semillas o frutas de plantas

grazes — eats grass
pastar — comer hierbas

hay — grass that is cut and dried for food
heno — hierba que se corta y se seca
para comida

shelter — something that covers or
protects
refugio — algo que cubre o protege

trot — to move at a pace between
walking and running
trotar — moverse a un paso entre caminar
y correr

For More Information/Más información

Books/Libros

A Field Full of Horses. Peter Hansard
   (Candlewick Press)

Great American Horses (series). Victor Gentle
   and Janet Perry (Gareth Stevens)

Horsepower: The Wonder of Draft Horses.
   Cris Peterson (Boyds Mills Press)

Horses! Gail Gibbons (Holiday House)

Web Sites/Páginas Web

Horses at Enchanted Learning
www.enchantedlearning.com/themes/horse.shtml
Rhymes and coloring printouts

23

Index/Índice

About the Author/Información sobre la autora

JoAnn Early Macken is the author of two rhyming picture books, *Sing-Along Song* and *Cats on Judy*, and four other series of nonfiction books for beginning readers. Her poems have appeared in several children's magazines. A graduate of the M.F.A. in Writing for Children and Young Adults program at Vermont College, she lives in Wisconsin with her husband and their two sons. Visit her Web site at www.joannmacken.com.

JoAnn Early Macken es autora de dos libros infantiles ilustrados en verso, *Sing-Along Song* y *Cats on Judy*, y también de cuatro series de libros de corte realista dirigidos a los lectores principiantes. Sus poemas han sido publicados en varias revistas para niños. Graduada del M.F.A. en Redacción para niños y adultos jóvenes del Vermont College, vive en Wisconsin con su esposo y sus dos hijos. Visita su página Web. www.joannmacken.com.